So, you to be a Wizard?

Poems
by
Wes Magee

Illustrations
by
Celia Gentles

First published in Great Britain in 2010
by Caboodle Books Ltd
Copyright © Wes Magee 2010

A Catalogue record for this book is available
from the British Library.

ISBN 9780 9565 239 14

Cover Illustration by Tom Truong
Inside Illustrations by Celia Gentles
Page Layout by Highlight Type Bureau Ltd
Printed by CPI Group (UK) Ltd, Croydon, CR0 4YY

The paper and board used in the paperback by
Caboodle Books Ltd are natural recyclable products
made from wood grown in sustainable forests.
The manufacturing processes conform to the environmental
regulations of the country of origin.

Caboodle Books Ltd
Riversdale, 8 Rivock Avenue, Steeton, BD20 6SA
www.authorsabroad.com

for
Barbara, Emma, Peter
and the Staff
at the Children's Discovery Centre, London

Books by Wes Magee

Poetry

Morning Break

The Witch's Brew

The Boneyard Rap

The Very Best of Wes Magee

The Phantom's Fang-tastic Show

The Ghost of the Grange

Fiction

Missing!

The Scribblers of Scumbagg School

The Scumbagg School Scorpion

Sports Day at Scumbagg School

The Spookspotters of Scumbagg School

The WinterWorld War

Blue, where are you?

Picture Books

The Legend of the Ragged Boy

Who Likes Pancakes?

Stroke the Cat

The Emperor and the Nightingale

Plays

It!

The Real Spirit of Christmas

Anthologies

The Puffin Book of Christmas Poems

Madtail Miniwhale & other shape poems

Dragon's Smoke

A Shooting Star

All through the Day

Contents

Giant

"Jack's killed the Giant!" That's what people said.
    Truth was, the fallen Ogre wasn't dead,
        but lay unconscious, huge lump on his head.
            He rose, when Jack and all had gone to bed.

With aching brain the Giant stomped away
    and walked the world for nine years and a day.
        Where mountains towered he stopped.
            "This looks okay,"
                he growled, and made his bed in boulder clay.

Hill climbers saw broad footprints now and then,
    but no one ever found the Giant's den.
        The people said, *"Beware! He'll come again,"*
            and left poor Jack to watch......
                and wonder when.

Who's Seen Jip?

Jip's run away,
left home for good.
I just *knew* he would
for earlier today
he was shouted at by Dad.
        "Bad dog!
                Bad dog!
                    Bad!"

Now Jip's a stray.
Where, *where* will he sleep?
I'm so sad I could weep.
Oh, doomsday, gloomsday
my dog has gone.

        Who's seen Jip?

                Anyone?

Justin Jefferson Jones

Up the stairs
and up the stairs
went Justin Jefferson Jones.
He heard a creak,
he heard a squeak,
he heard some grumbling groans.
He heard a sigh,
he heard a cry,
he heard some mumbling moans
did Justin Jefferson,
      Justin Jefferson,
            Justin Jefferson Jones.

Down the stairs
and down the stairs
ran Justin Jefferson Jones.
"Mum, what a scare
I had up there!
I heard some ghostly groans!
I heard a wheeze,
I heard a sneeze,
I heard some rattling bones!"
cried Justin Jefferson,
      Justin Jefferson,
            Justin Jefferson Jones.

Mum shook her head.
She laughed, and said,
"Justin Jefferson Jones,
you silly man,
that's only Gran
*on her **two** mobile 'phones!*
To bed upstairs,
and no more scares,
and no more rattling bones,
my Justin Jefferson,
         Justin Jefferson,
                  Justin Jefferson Jones!"

Football Dreaming

I'm
a striker racing,
a fullback chasing,
a winger crossing,
a captain bossing,
a wingback tackling,
a stopper shackling,
a halfback strolling,
a coach controlling,
a forward flicking,
a goalie kicking,
a linkman scheming,
a mad fan dreaming
   on
     the
       morning
         bus
           to
             school.

The Wembley Way

One sunny Saturday in May
we joined the crowds on Wembley Way.

We joined the fans all strolling up
to watch the Final of the Cup.

We saw huge banners help up high
and saw flags fly against the sky.

The fans all joked and larked about
And *"Wembley! Wembley!"* was the shout.

"Come on you Blues!" "Come on you Reds!"
We saw tall coloured hats on heads.

Both sets of fans let laughter ring,
and you should just have heard them sing.

There was no nastiness, just fun,
as all the fans smiled in the sun.

The game was great. Ten out of ten!
But nothing matched the friendship when

up for the Cup on Final Day
we joined the crowds on Wembley Way.

So, you want to be a Wizard?

So, you want to be a wizard?
    Well, you'll need a pointed hat
    with silver stars and golden moon,
    and perched on top…..a bat.

So, you want to be a wizard?
    Well, you'll need *'Ye Booke of Spells'*,
    six rotten eggs, and fried frogs legs
    to make revolting smells.

So, you want to be a wizard?
    Well, you'll need some pickled brains,
    a wand, a cloak, one headless rat,
    and green slime from the drains.

Do you *still* want to be a wizard?

Witch Nastee Spella's
Hallowe'en Party Stew

As Witch Nastee stirred
her black cat purred
and the cauldron popped and bubbled.
The vile blue stew
looked as thick as glue.
The guests felt, *er*, rather troubled.

Nastee dropped in ants,
old underpants,
and holly shaped in a wreath.
One cob of corn,
a stifled yawn,
and her set of blackened false teeth.

She plopped in keys,
skinned knobbly knees,
plus a splodge of tomato sauce.
Hairs from a dog,
some rancid frog
and the shoe from a cowboy's horse.

Thick was the smoke
(it made the guests choke!)
but the Witch was pleased with her brew.
    She chucked in figs
    and innards of pigs
to create her Hallowe'en Stew.

"Come on, you lot,
taste from the pot
or I'll turn you all into mice!"
    The guests dipped in,
    one elf *slipped* in,
and agreed it was, *er,* rather nice!

They gobbled and grabbed,
they swallowed and blabbed.
The guests' manners were *so* crude and rude.
    All of them slurped,
    and most of them burped
as they guzzled the party food.

Yeeeuuuggghhh - cious!

Rover!

All the guests have gone home
to Deal, Diss, and Dover.
Our house looks like a tip
now the party is over.
Time to call in our dog,
rough and ravenous Rover.

He devours all the scraps
cast aside by the ravers:
sausage ends, curried rice,
and crushed crisps of all flavours.
Rover wolfs down the lot:
kebabs, kumquats, and Quavers.

That dog's a devourer.
He's our household improver.
Prawns, peanuts, and prunes gulped
by our rubbish remover.
Rover's tongue sweeps each rug:
he's one huge, hairy hoover.

An Invitation to the Vampire's *'Bite Fright'* Party

You're invited to my *'Bite Fright'*
to be held at Castle Krekk.
Only prezzies I'll accept, right,
are cash, credit card, or cheque.

Wear top hat, long cloak, and black boots.
Both fangs *must* be tipped with red.
'Drax Snax' have promised pickled newts.
There'll be music by *'The Dead'*.

You'll be served iced blood in moonlight
by my butler, E'zza Wrekk.
Gory games kick-off at midnight
with that old fave, *'Bite-Yer-Neck'*.

And, please, no fighting or disputes
…. or you might just lose your head.
'Bite Fright' ends when Screech Owl hoots,
then it's back to coffin bed….
      "Ahhhhhhhhhhhhhhhhhhh!"

Yours bloodsuckingly,

I.M.A. Vampire.   BA(d). ON(e).

PS: *Don't be late for this A+ date!*

<u>*Information Note:*</u> **BA(d)** - **B**loodthirsty **A**ristocrat (class '**d**')
      ON(e) - **O**rder of the **N**ight (grade '**e**')

17

The Worst Girl in the School

She's crop-haired, she's scowly,
and at football she's tough.
Wears ripped jeans, scuffed trainers,
and looks really rough.
If she loses at netball
she throws one huge huff.
    She's naughty,
    she's warty,
    but she's no piece of fluff
    is Gwendoline
        Gertie
            Griselda
                MacGruff.

She's raw-boned, she's muscly,
she's a bit of a scruff.
She ignores referees
when they shout, *"No rough stuff!"*
In ice-cold December
she swims in the buff.
    She's loudest,
    she's proudest,
    but she's no piece of fluff
    is Gwendoline
        Gertie
            Griselda
                MacGruff.

The Supply Teacher's Prayer

"Oh, tomorrow,
let them all be clean and neat,
let no one head-butt, lie or cheat,
let none come in with dog-fouled feet.
    Oh, and *please,*
don't let them taunt, or trick, or tease.
    Please!"

"Oh, tomorrow,
let them all sit still, be calm,
let no one Chinese-burn an arm,
let none set off the fire alarm.
    Oh, and *please,*
don't let them shout, or spit, or sneeze.
    Please!"

"Oh, tomorrow,
let them all be smiley nice,
let no one swear – *at any price!* –
let's not find fleas or nits or lice.
    Oh, and *please,*
no flowing blood from nose, or knees.
    Please!
        Please!!"

What's Behind the Green Curtain?

> "No! No! No!"

That's our Head teacher going on and on and on
at morning assembly in the Hall.
Bored, I stare at the green curtain
hanging behind him on the wall
.....and *wonder*
behind that green curtain
could there be
a mini Mercurian with eyes on its toes,
or a non-smoking dragon with a code dinnis doze....?

> *"In this school there'll be*
> *no fighting,*
> *no thumping,*
> *no punching,*
> *no clumping!"*

I *wonder*.....
behind that green curtain
could there be
a ravenous ogre devouring an ox,
or a fox in a box, in a box, in a box.....?

> *"In this school there'll be*
> *no kicking,*
> *no clouting,*
> *no kissing,*
> *no shouting!"*

I *wonder*…..
behind that green curtain
could there be
a menacing monster with worms on its face,
or simply an empty and echoing space…….?

> *"In this school there'll be*
> *no running,*
> *no dreaming,*
> *no spitting,*
> *no scream -!"*

When…..suddenly, a **hand**,
 a huge,
   hairy,
      horrible,
        horrendous
     hand
        appears,
grabs our Head teacher
and hauls him behind the green curtain!
We gaze amazed,
then realise he's gone,
he's gone…. for certain!

He's gone!
No fuss.
No mess.
We jump up,
punch the air,
and shout,

"YESSSSSSSSSSS!!!"

Crocodiles

(an acrostic)

Crocodiles
are Really cunning fighters.
With monstrOus jaws
and Crushing teeth
they're awesOme biters.
Like Dead tree trunks
they float In swamps,
waiting for Lunch.
Then they'll suddEnly attack.
Snap! Crunch!

An Alligator I saw in Florida

"I'm full of fish.
Ummm, feel quite replete.
Now what could be better
than to dangle my feet
in cool, cool water?
Hey, man,
this is
really,
really
neat!"

"I'm watchful, though.
My slit-eyed gaze
warns I'm not *totally* lost
in day-dreamy haze.
On this mud-bank I bask.
Hey, man,
I love
these
loooooong
lazeeeeeee
days!"

23

Frogs in Springtime

Suddenly, they're back in the pond,
the *'Frog Choir'*
at top volume croak.
And *what* a crowd!

A ray of sunshine, like a baton,
conducts a frog chorus
that is deep and low
and long and loud.

All around the World there's Weather

There's a rainbow over Russia,
  golden rays are toasting Spain,
far Taiwan's beset by typhoons,
  England is awash with rain.

Sandstorms sweep the dry Sahara,
  Scottish hills are lost in mist,
thunder booms above the tropics,
  Singapore is sunshine-kissed.

All around the world there's weather,
pressure high or pressure low.
Vast black clouds or brilliant sunsets,
whirlwinds wild or silent snow.

Howling gales sweep down from Iceland,
  winter Wales has sleet and storm,
blizzards rage across the Arctic,
  but Brazil is wet and warm.

Ireland is the land of drizzle
  - fields in forty shades of green.
Hurricanes roar through the U.S.
  and have names like Joe or Jean.

All around the world there's weather,
pressure high or pressure low.
Vast black clouds or brilliant sunsets,
whirlwinds wild or silent snow.

The Music of the Wind

     The wind
     makes **LOUD** music.
It roars above the rooftops,
it drums beneath the floor,
it howls around the gable-end
and rat-a-tats the door.

     The wind
     makes *quiet* music.
It whistles down the chimney,
it tiptoes through a tree,
it hums against the windowpane
and whispers tunes to me.

Amy's Harp

Amy calls
    her harp
        'The Tree of Strings',

and when
    she plays
        it sings, it sings!

When the Funfair Comes to Town

See the coloured lights that flash,
hear the dodgems when they crash,
give the coconuts a bash
    when the Funfair comes to town,
        when the Funfair comes to town.

Smell the burgers, peas and pies,
wear a mask with wobbly eyes,
throw a hoop and win a prize
    when the Funfair comes to town,
        when the Funfair comes to town.

See the crowds come in and out,
hear the children squeal and shout,
climb aboard the roundabout
    when the Funfair comes to town,
        when the Funfair comes to town.

Taste the toffee you can share,
hear loud music in the air,
ride the Ghost Train.....if you dare
    when the Funfair comes to town,
        when the Funfair comes to town.

Pleasant Scents

The kitchen just before lunch on Christmas Day....
Salty-spray when waves crash on rocks in the bay....
In school, when you model with clammy, damp clay....
Pleasant scents
that stay with you
for ever.

The attic's dry air after days of June heat.....
A shower of Spring rain that refreshes the street.....
An orange you peel: the tang sharp, yet so sweet.....
Pleasant scents
that stay with you
for ever.

The Bonfire Night smoke as it drifts in the dark....
Air lemony-clean on the Island of Sark.....
Mint in the back garden.... and mud in the park.....
Pleasant scents
that stay with you
for ever.

Great Independence Day!

Today was Independence Day,
  the Fourth day of July.
Dad put up the 'Stars and Stripes'
  and mum baked apple pie.
I wore my cowboy boots and hat.
  The sun shone in the sky.

We held a square dance on the lawn.
  Those fiddlers! They could play!
We ate our fill of hot dogs
  as we sat on bales of hay.
That night I flopped in bed and said,
  "Great Independence Day!"

The Hairdresser's Questions

"So, tell me,
do you want it crimped,
or do you want it curled?
Do you want it styled or wild,
or do you want it twirled?
Do you want a 'Grizzly Bear'?
    Tell me,
      tell me,
        tell me
          tell me,
how *do* you want your hair?"

                  "Er......er......"

"So, tell me,
do you want it gelled,
or do you want it fringed?
Do you want it fluffed or roughed,
or do you want it singed?
Do you want a 'Hedgehog Scare'?
    Tell me,
      tell me,
        tell me,
          tell me,
how *do* you want your hair?"

          "Er......er......"

Skin Magic

That cooling hand placed on your hot brow….
Your toes when they're tickled by fingers….
When someone you love just touches your arm….
      Ahhhhh,
      skin magic
      that lingers
      and lingers….

The time when you walked hand in hand on a beach….
That hug when you felt, *oh,* so tragic….
The brush of soft lips on your tear-stained cheek….
      Ahhhhh,
      pure moments
      of magic,
      skin magic …..

One Day?

One day
we'll land on planet Mars.

One day
we'll travel to the stars.

One day
we'll live upon the Moon.

This year?

Next year?

One day?

Soon?

The Solar System Tour

"Climb aboard! Yes, climb board!
You'll have a lifetime's thrill!
You'll love the Solar System Tour.
　　We know,
　　we *know* you will!"

"We'll whizz you right round Saturn,
then Mercury, then Mars!
See Venus *and* see Neptune!
　　You'll spot
　　a *million* stars!"

"Jupiter and Uranus!
Pluto, our Earth *and* Moon!
So, climb aboard the spaceship.
　　Be quick!
　　We're leaving soon!"

The Sniffle

(an alien....... from Saturn)

The Sniffle's massive nose
is redder than a rose,
and on its plastic toes
there is a paint that glows.
It eats fried eggs at Joe's
and chips that once were froze.
It then sings Yo-Ho-Ho's
while sitting in repose.
When biting cold wind blows
you'll see it strike a pose:
it stands like that, I s'pose,
because it wears no clo'se.
It likes to list its woes
in rhyme, rather than prose,
then much prefers to doze
in lengths of garden hose.
The Sniffle's one of those
daft floating so-and-so's,
and sings like choirs of crows

as

off

through

Space

it

goes.

The Never-Seen-Before

Long, long before first life forms,
when the Earth was red and raw,
time-travellers stopped-off here
on their way to Alpha Four.
  Metal-clad and monstrous were
    the *Never-Seen-Before*.

They loved Earth's vast volcanoes,
so with iron-clanging roar
they crawled down the central vents
to the planet's molten core.
  Hades-hot and heavy were
    the *Never-Seen-Before*.

Then when our planet cooled down
and rains began to pour,
the *N-S-Bs* turned rusty
so took-off for Alpha Four.
  Never seen again were
    the *Never-Seen-Before*.

Today, in dead volcanoes,
vulcanologists explore
and stumble on a neck bolt
or a curved metallic claw:
  the only relics left by
    the *Never-Seen-Before*.

Holiday Trip.... in the 22nd Century

You'll take a break on Venus
- it's lava-hot in June,
then join an all-night party
on the dark side of the Moon.

You'll sail through storms on Saturn,
and trudge the sands of Mars,
then zoom away to Neptune
and tour some distant stars.

You'll skate on icy Pluto
and ski for all your worth,
then when the hols are over

    you'll

       fly

          back

            home

        to

             Earth.

Visiting a Ruined Castle in Scotland

The narrow, snaking path
leads us to a ruined castle
perched precariously on a cliff top.
It's a steaming day in July.
    Perfect weather.
Glancing back we see the mountains,
sky high,
    and purple with heather.

We idle across a courtyard
where wild flowers bloom between flagstones,
then peer down a dry well.
Walking the battlements
    takes an hour
before we find spiral stairs:
uneven stone steps lead us
    up the tower.

At the top there's a circular room
curtained with cobwebs.
Sunlight spears through slit windows
and illuminates dust.
    Motes turning, flashing.
Far, far below the sea is foaming:
against jagged rocks waves
    are crashing.

It was here, in this stone room,
the Highland clansman made his last stand.
Here he fended off 'Butcher' Cumberland's troops
with blood-stained claymore
    flailing.
He died. Legend says he returns at midnight,
weeping for his lost Scotland:
    wailing.

No one's scared by such a ghost story,
or by this deserted, crumbling ruin
on a sweltering day in July.
There's nothing left to see
    but stone.
But *who* would stay here in this tower room
and await the midnight hour
    .....*alone?*

Who?

Me?

You?

The Annual Sack Race at
'Worst Ever School'

As we set off and race
　　we are all filled with fear
　　　　for we know where these sacks
　　　　　　have been stored since last year.
　　　　　　　　They've been down in the cellar,
　　　　　　piled on dusty old racks,
　　　　and hundreds of creatures
　　have made homes
in these sacks.

There are.....
　　ants, weevils, midges,
　　　　fat spiders and slugs,
　　　　　　bluebottles, dust mites,
　　　　　　　　big earwigs and bugs.
　　　　　　There are.....centipedes, horse flies,
　　　　wasps, hornets and bees,
　　ticks, millipedes, moths,
cockroaches and fleas.

How we itch, how we scratch,
　　how we jump in the sacks
　　　　as scores of feared crawlies
　　　　　　creep right up our backs.
　　　　　　　　We collapse in a heap
　　　　　　and we're not
　　　　really cool
　　in the Annual Sack Race
at *'Worst Ever School'*.

 40

The Class Teacher's Ghost Speaks....
to his Pupils

"For making me tear out my hair,
   for drawing pins left on my chair,
      for calling me Old Grumpy Bear
         I'll be spooking you.....

"For all the tiresome tricks you played,
   for rotten stink bomb smells you made,
      for rank bad manners you displayed
         I'll be spooking you.....

"For rude things drawn on wall and door,
   for muddy kit on cloakroom floor,
      for all your ceaseless jaw jaw jaw
         I'll be spooking you.....

"For rumours, lies, and tales you told,
   for all your dreadful jokes – *so old!* –
      for giving me your cough and cold
         I'll be spooking you.....

41

"For making fun of my big ears,
    for playground fights that end in tears,
        for all the headaches down the years
            I'll be spooking you......

"For all who thought it fun to shout
    or squeal or spit or clown or clout,
        you'd best beware, you'd best watch out
            for – *yes, indeed!* –
                be in no doubt,
                    I'll be spooking you......"

Seagulls

The seagulls glide
above the town.
We throw out scraps
and they swoop down.
     One seagull,
       two seagulls,
         three seagulls,
         four!
With a shriek
  and a squawk
   here come

more,

   more,

     more!

Garden Birds........ Beware!

4 pigeons flutter down for bread.

6 seagulls glide high overhead.

5 sparrows peck at tiny crumbs.

1 robin in the winter comes.

3 swallows don't stay here too long.

2 blackbirds sing their evening song.

And.....in the bushes.....lying flat,

there lurks **1** hungry ginger cat.

The Bag Lady of *'The Lodge'*

Daily we saw her, a bent old lady
with carrier bags in both hands,
trudging back to *'The Lodge'*,
her vast, mysterious mansion
half-lost in overgrown gardens.
      There she lived alone.

One chill November night
we ventured up the gravel path,
our torches glimmering on ghost trees.
Hidden in rustling bushes
we spied on the darkened *'Lodge'*.
      No sign of life.

For a dare we hurled stones
at the silent house.
One ricocheted off the wall,
one clattered down the slate roof,
and the third arced in moonlight
      …..then smashed a window!

That tinkling sound – and an owl's cry –
sent us racing away
in heart-thudding panic.
We charged past the rusty iron gates
and on up the frosty road.
      Moonbeams fingered us: guilty.

Now, when I hear the sound
of breaking glass, I shudder
and relive the agony
of that scary winter's night,
and how we beset the old lady
      of *'The Lodge'*.

The Peasants' Revolt, 1381

There was a grumbling in the land
and soon the peasants were revolting.
    In their hordes they massed for battle
    but, alas, smelled just like cattle.
    Most were dandruffy and toothless
    as in rags they fought the ruthless.
    The poor peasants, pock-marked, potty,
    were all scabby-legged and spotty.
They came in cart-loads, sick with jolting,
Oh yes,
    the peasants *were* revolting.

There was a mumbling in the land
and soon the peasants were revolting.
    Armed with scythes and pitchforks (rusty)
    they were dirty, drunk, and dusty.
    Grimy hands hurled stones and boulders.
    Nitty hair hung to their shoulders.
    The sad peasants, squint-eyed, shabby,
    were as thin as rakes, or flabby.
Their goatskin coats were patched, some moulting.
Oh yes,
    the peasants *were* revolting.

Sir Robert Peel's 'Peelers'

(founded in 1829)

Sir Robert Peel's 'Peelers'
nicked robbers and stealers,
put away shady dealers
    in old London,
        old London Town.

At Inns like *'O'Malley's'*
and down gloomy alleys
'Peelers' scared off the scallies
    in old London,
        old London Town.

The 'Peelers' got shirty
when bad girls were flirty
with Lord Digby-Dirty
    in old London,
        old London Town.

They chased all the bad lads,
and locked-up rough footpads
who'd mugged bewigged grandads
    in old London,
        old London Town.

 48

Smugglers' Moon

Tonight, a full moon
unrolls its golden carpet
across the silver sea.

A Spoonful of Sugar

Someone has spilled
a spoonful of sugar
across the polished walnut table,
and thousands of white grains
sparkle and shine on the dark wood.
     Nearby, in a fruit bowl,
     lies a yellow banana
     with bruises like mini craters.

It reminds me of last night
as we ran home after the party,
and saw, far above,
a cratered crescent moon
and thousands of twinkling stars.
     It was as if someone had spilled
     a spoonful of sugar
     across the night sky.

Diwali! Diwali!

Diwali! Diwali!
Light the lamps
right now!

Let the flames so small and bright
guide us through the darkest night.
Let the flames so small and bright
lead us safely to the light.

Diwali! Diwali!
Light the lamps
right now!

Voices........

"Come in!"
My mother's voice boomed across the backs of houses
calling me home as dusk fell that July evening.
But still we stayed, four friends adventuring
at the end of Matthew's long, overgrown garden
where a tumbledown shed, marooned in waves of weeds,
was our pirate ship sailing uncharted seas.
Dirt-streaked, and oblivious to the deepening purple dark,
we played on as first stars blinked like harbour lights.
"Come in!
It's late!
Come in!"

"Come in!"
The boatman's hoarse shout reverberated
across the lake's sparkling, sunlit-wrinkled water.
Yet my cousins and I continued to row towards the reed
beds
where ducks, moorhens and coots paddled and pecked.
We laughed as heavy oars dipped and splashed,
and gazed when a flight of geese took off, wings clapping.
The rowing boat rocked in the wind and waves,
and still the boatman's hand-cupped call from the jetty,
"Come in!
Time's up!
Come in!"

52

"Come in!"
The bent old woman smiled toothlessly
as she invited the children lost in the green wood
to rest in her cottage hidden amidst bushes and trees.
I remember how the storyteller added scary sound effects
- an owl's wavering hoot, wind hushing in the treetops,
and his fingers snapping like dead, woodland twigs.
Dry-mouthed and wide-eyed we stared intently
as he mimicked the witch's final invitation,
   "Come in,
         dear children.
               Come in!"

The Twenty Steps to the Cellar

You descend with trepidation,
    one stone step at a time,
      your torch illuminating
walls draped with 'webs and grime.
 Down this same foot-worn stairway,
        for centuries gone by,
   tramped scullions and kitchen-maids
        came servants with a sigh
      to dump unwanted chattels
     by gleam of flick'ring lamp
     on the cellar's cold flagstones
       amidst the rising damp.
  And now their shades surround you,
       throng the sweet-sour air,
     trailing shrouds of memories
     that touch and wisp your hair,
     but you must keep descending
       a step, then one step more
       until at last you stand upon
        the cellar's flagstone floor.

Coal Fire in December

It's great,
in icy December,
to get home
and chuck off
coat, gloves,
boots, scarf
        and hat,

and, *ahhhhh,*
sit in front
of a glowing coal fire
and hear the warmth
purrrrrrrrrrrr
like a contented
        cat.

December in Thorgill

(Thorgill is a tiny hamlet high on the North York Moors)

Tipsy, the frothed gill
stumbles over stones.
Sheep bleat in sleet
  on the moor's cold shoulder.
High above the iced pond
a hungry heron unfurls
like a blue flag,
  and the fox grows bolder,
        bolder,
          bolder,
            bolder.

Owls haunt the wood,
while small birds squabble
at the food-station
  of a peanut-holder.
There's fire frost and chill wind
as snow clouds gather
over Rosedale Moor
  and December days grow colder,
        colder,
          colder,
            colder.

gill: *a fast-flowing, moorland stream*

Starfall

Exploded stars,
   cosmos swirled,
     each winter fall
       upon our world.

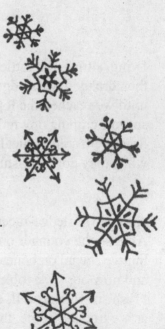

This dust of stars,
   weightless, white,
     drifts down and settles
       in the night.

We wake to find
   the fields aglow,
     and wrongly call
       this starfall.......snow.

The Super Sledging Stars

A long, hard winter. Snow lay deep and soft.
Sledges appeared from cellar, shed and loft.
We duffled-up from head to booted feet
and, with all the traffic stilled, reclaimed our street.
We made a slide that glinted like a gun,
and sledged non-stop on our own Cresta Run.

Lying, sitting, we rattled down the slope
then dragged our sledges back on reins of rope
until we reached the top. Then off we'd go
speed-bumping down the track of hard-packed snow.
Some fell, some squealed; the hopeless ones got miffed
when they got head-stuck in a roadside drift.

All day we sledge-raced down that icy slide.
At dusk the younger ones were called inside,
but we stayed on beneath the streetlights' beam
and now our slide took on a silver gleam.
Fresh snowflakes fell, enshrouding roadside cars,
as we trudged home, the super sledging stars.

A New Set of Christmas Lights

There are twenty
brand-new fairy lights
draped around
our Christmas tree.
They are a very
special gift
that Gran
has sent to me.

Each little light
is star-shaped.
Switch them on
- oh, *what* a sight!
There's a brand-new
constellation
shining brightly
in the night!

This Silent Night

(......on the North York Moors)

Bathed in the back door's yellow light
you gaze upon a winter's night

and view the shy Moon's misty veil
as car beams flick across the dale.

A black cat pads the patio
to leave small paw-prints in the snow,

and air's aglitter, stars are bright
   this Christmas Eve,
      this silent night.

The Christmas Shed

It was late afternoon on Christmas Day
with light fading and flakes falling
when the three of us raced through the copse
where rhododendrons and holly bushes
bent low under their burden of fresh snow.
Gasping, we skidded to a stop
at the edge of the estate's allotments.
A bitter, whining wind made us shiver
as it whipped across the frozen earth.
>   *"No one's about.*
>   *Come on!"*

Slipping and skating we dashed for Jacko's shed
and at the back crawled through a hole
where the old boards had rotted away.
Inside it was dry. The air was still.
We peered as daylight filtered dimly
through the fly-spattered, cobwebbed window,
and breathed the shed's special smell
of pine, creosote, paraffin, and sawdust.
Fear of discovery made us whisper.
>   *"Let's see if they're*
>   *still there."*

Carefully we moved garden implements
that were stacked in a corner.
Dried soil fell and crunched beneath our boots
as we shifted rakes, forks, spades, and hoes,
and *there* was Smoky and her four kittens
warm in a bed of worn gloves and jerseys.
Like the Three Kings we knelt and offered
our Christmas gifts – turkey scraps, ham, a sausage.
Smoky arched and purred and ate hungrily.
　　　"The kittens
　　　　　are still blind."

The food vanished. We watched in silence
as the grey cat lay down and her mewling kittens
guzzled greedily at the milk bar.
　　　"It's late."
　　　　　We replaced the implements
and crept out of Jacko's old shed.
Like shadows we hared for the cover of the copse.
Chilled to the bone we reached our estate
where Christmas lights were flashing. We split.
　　　"Same time tomorrow?"
　　　　"Yeah."
　　　　　"See you."

A Thinking Christmas

A turkey dinner
at Christmas is great.

Think.....
somewhere a boy
with an empty plate.

The Christmas tree lights
shine red, green and gold.

Think.....
somewhere a girl
shivering and cold.

Presents and parties!
Yes, *that's* Christmas Day.

Think.....
somewhere a child
asleep in the hay.

Wes Magee

is an award winning children's author
who has published more than 100 books,
including poetry, fiction, plays, picture books
and anthologies.
'The Very Best of Wes Magee' (poems)
won the Children's Poetry Bookshelf Award,
and **'Madtail Minwhale & other shape poems'**
was a Puffin Books bestseller.

A CD of his poems is available from The Poetry Archive.
His work has been filmed for TV,
and featured many times on radio.

When not travelling nationwide to visit schools
where he performs his 'Poetry Show'
and runs writing workshops,
Wes lives in a tiny hamlet on the Yorkshire Wolds.
He has 3 pets – Maya and Bubble (dogs)
and Tinkerbelle (a cat).